COOKING WITH
TURMERIC

This Wind-Up Books edition published in 2018
by Elwin Street Productions Limited

Copyright English Edition © Elwin Street Productions Limited, 2018

Conceived and produced by
Elwin Street Productions Limited
14 Clerkenwell Green
London EC1R 0DP
www.elwinstreet.com

ISBN 978-1-911130-69-7

10 9 8 7 6 5 4 3 2 1

Originally published under the title: Curcuma, en cuisine by Garance Leureux © 2010
by Éditions La Plage, Paris

Translator: Drew Smith

Picture Credits:
Photographs by Fabrice Subiros and styling by Emmanuel Renault,
except Alamy: © Westend61 GmbH / Alamy Stock Photo, front cover; Picture Pantry:
© Natalia Klenova, back cover; Shutterstock: © Pikoso.kz, 2; © tarapong srichaiyos, 8;
© mics, 11; © Emily Li, 15; © xuanhuongho, 17; © Lifestyle_Studio, 18; © SiNeeKan,
25; © Anna_Pustynnikova, 32; © Wealthylady, 42; © Larisa Blinova, 52; © Kencana
Studio, 60; © zkruger, 65; © Kiian Oksana, 66; © elisekurenbina, 79.

Printed in China

COOKING WITH
TURMERIC

superfood recipes to enrich your diet
and boost your health

Garance Leureux

CONTENTS

CHAPTER 4
Cakes, pancakes and curries

CHAPTER 5
Desserts, sweets and sorbets

ONE

DISCOVER

Used in India for thousands of years as a spice and
medicinal herb, turmeric is not only rich in flavour,
but has a variety of health benefits. A natural
superfood with powerful antioxidant properties, it
also contains nutrients such as manganese and iron,
and can help prevent both heart disease and cancer.

THE MAGIC OF TURMERIC

Turmeric – *Curcuma longa* in Latin – belongs to the same family as ginger, cardamom and galangal. Its vivid orange root has been cultivated since the earliest days of Asian civilisation, where it was used as a spice, a rub and a medicine.

Indeed, turmeric has been put to an impressive list of uses through time, from clothing dye – adding colour to the robes of Buddhist monks – to ceremonial blessing, annointing the foreheads of newborn babies in India. It has even been used as an animal-pelt deodorant.

In health

Wherever turmeric has grown, it has found its way into the medicine chest. It is prescribed for digestive complaints and – with its disinfectant properties – makes a soothing salve for wounds. In Ayurvedic medicine it is regarded as a powerful antiseptic.

More recently, turmeric has been the focus of much research, as a potential treatment for Alzheimer's disease, cancer and other diseases, especially of the skin. Its influence on cognitive functions, blood-sugar balance and kidney function is also being investigated to the full.

This much is for certain: cooking vegetables with turmeric helps them retain their beta-carotene content. Furthermore, turmeric is low in cholesterol and sodium, and a great source of vitamins C and B6, magnesium, iron, potassium and manganese. Even taken in small quantities over time, turmeric is thought to possess powerful anti-inflammatory properties.

In the kitchen

Piperine, the active spicy element in pepper, boosts the effects of turmeric, so I have used pepper throughout this book. When I say a grind or two, I do mean a generous grind or two rather than just a pinch. Also, where I use just a teaspoon, there is no harm – in fact, there are palpable benefits – in upping the quantity to a tablespoon if it is to your taste.

In the kitchen, turmeric usually appears in mixes – in Indian or Thai curries, in masalas and in mukhwas, in the mix of spices Indians eat at the end of a meal to aid digestion, and also in Caribbean gumbos and North African ras el hanout. Turmeric gives them all colour and vibrancy, and preserves their goodness too. In Europe and America, turmeric provides the yellow colouring of mustard but it also appears in other guises – ice cream, cake and sauces. In these dishes, it is listed under the moniker of E100.

To appreciate the many wonderful qualities of turmeric – its warm tone, its peppery flavour, even its hint of acorn and butternut – we need to start in the kitchen.

ROOT AND POWDER

Much of the turmeric you'll find on sale in Europe originates from southern India (Kerala), China, Réunion Island and Madagascar. The root grows in countries with a tropical monsoon climate, prone to heavy rainfall for up to six months.

Turmeric's most basic form is that of a root, resembling ginger but a little smaller. Fresh turmeric is easy to find in Asian shops, but a little less readily available on supermarket shelves – despite its growing popularity as a star ingredient in healthly modern cuisine. Shop for roots that are firm, but a little juicy when cut. You can treat fresh turmeric like ginger and mince it finely, or even put it through a garlic press – just watch out for your hands and work surfaces as the root can stain even more than the powder. For this reason alone, powdered turmeric is easier to handle! To make this powder, fresh roots are boiled and dried in the sunshine wherever they've been harvested, then crushed, ground and stored in dark, dry conditions to conserve their rich antioxidant content. As a general rule, the fresher the turmeric, the more potent the smell and the colour.

Just remember that colour can vary quite considerably according to the turmeric's country of origin – so colour is not the only criterion for quality. Organic is best, of course, and always buy in small sachets that won't be left languishing in the back of your cupboard – where it could lose its healthy potency. For most of the recipes you'll find in this book, root and powder are interchangeable, but powder is generally easier.

Organic turmeric and fair trade

Most turmeric is grown on small farms that function as co-operatives. It's common for turmeric to be twinned with another crop, such as tea. Organic and fair trade are good marks of quality because they both conform to Kitemark standards, meaning that the turmeric is not adulterated with colourants, as is often the case with saffron. Some wholesalers will import the roots whole and grind them after they are delivered to be sure of the quality.

FRIENDS OF TURMERIC

Turmeric's benefits are enhanced when combined with a range of other ingredients. Pair with any of the foods below – all of which are loaded with the micro-nutrients our bodies need to defend against cancer and various other diseases – for meals that deliver an incredible nutritional hit, doubling, if not tripling, turmeric's potential.

Flaxseed

Also known as linseeds, flaxseeds are sold in two varieties: white and brown. They are rich in omega 3 (making them a perfect choice for vegans) as well as antioxidants. Blitz them in a coffee or spice grinder for maximum absorption. Alternatively you can buy them pre-ground and ready to eat. If you do decide to grind your own, it is best to do so in small batches so that the seeds don't oxidise. Use them in recipes that don't require any heating. Flaxseeds also make a great natural laxative. Simply soak the seeds overnight to make them more digestible.

Flaxseed oil should be stored in the dark in an opaque bottle or tin. Once opened, be sure to use quickly to prevent the oil from oxidising. Traditionally flaxseed oil is eaten with breakfast. Two teaspoons with your porridge or muesli makes for a healthy start to the day.

Ginger

Turmeric and ginger are closely related, and alike in more than just appearance. Ginger's properties as a stimulant and aphrodisiac are well known. Nowadays it's being studied for its potential to help combat cancer, thanks to its antioxidant constituent, gingerol. For optimum nutritional benefit, be sure to shop for fresh roots that – as with turmeric – should be firm to the touch, not wrinkled, and slightly moist when cut. Peel off the skin and mince, or use a garlic press. You can also grate the ginger, or slice it thinly, to make an infusion (see page 28).

Agave

More than just an ingredient in tequila, agave is a sweet syrup that makes a great alternative to sugar. The fructose in it only has a mild effect on your glycaemic index and this is not the only reason to opt for agave over sugar. Agave gives oven-baked cakes a gorgeous syrupy texture, melts quickly when used to sweeten ice creams and sorbets and has a neutral flavour that combines easily with fruits.

Shiitake mushrooms

The benefits of eating shiitake mushrooms are common knowledge in China and Japan. Earthy and flavoursome, these mushrooms are guaranteed to boost your immune system. In dried form, they are convenient to cook with. Simply cut off any hard roots and rehydrate in a bowl of boiled water. When they have swelled up – in 15 to 20 minutes' time – take them out, drain and prepare as you would any other mushroom (see on toast, page 38, or cabbage soup, page 48). And be sure not to throw away the water that you soaked them in. This stock can be used as the basis for soup or broth.

Tofu

Tofu is derived from soya milk, curdled and pressed into solid blocks. The milk consists of yellow soya beans mixed with a coagulant such as nigari. Rich in protein, tofu is a healthy substitute for both meat and dairy products; swap it into your favourite recipes to make them instantly suitable for vegans. When smoked, tofu takes on an almost bacon-like consistency (see the cauliflower curry with prunes on page 64). Silken tofu, which has the consistency of a flan, can work in both sweet and savoury dishes (see agave, lemon and turmeric sorbet on page 74). It absorbs other flavours well and can win over even the most sceptical of meat-eaters (see mustard tofu with spicy pumpkin purée on page 62).

OTHER USES FOR TURMERIC

With its myriad health benefits, turmeric makes a great addition to your diet but there are other ways that you can utilize this wonder spice. See below for just a selection of spicy suggestions.

Dry skin: Turmeric – or *haldi* as it's called in India – is an ingredient in many traditional beauty recipes and particularly effective for treating dry skin. Mix a teaspoon of turmeric with a tablespoon of honey and apply gently to your face. Leave for ten minutes and then rinse.

Joint pain relief: Thanks to its strong anti-inflammatory properties turmeric is a traditional treatment for arthritis and osteoporosis – in Ayurvedic and Chinese herbal medicine. Curcumin is the active ingredient responsible for turmeric's anti-inflammatory action and curcumin extract is now widely available. However, these supplements are not suitable for everyone so consult your doctor before taking.

Scalp treatment: Turmeric mixed with olive oil is a natural dandruff remedy, which has been around for centuries. Mix turmeric and olive oil (coconut oil also works nicely) and massage gently into your scalp. Leave for ten to fifteen minutes and then wash your hair as normal.

Settle upset stomachs: There's no better way to settle the symptoms of an upset stomach than with a turmeric tea or infusion (see page 28), particularly when it's infused with ginger. This home remedy has been around for centuries, and many people still swear by its soothing properties today.

Smooth skin: To soften your skin and exfoliate dead, dry cells, try a zingy turmeric scrub. Mix turmeric powder and rolled oats with a little water until you have a thick paste. Use this paste regularly as a body scrub to brighten, buff and polish your skin.

Stretch marks: Historically turmeric has been used as a natural and simple way of reducing the appearance of stretch marks. Mix one teaspoon of turmeric with a tablespoon or two of natural yoghurt, apply to the affected area. Leave on for ten to fifteen minutes. Rinse with warm water. Repeat twice daily until the marks fade.

TWO

OILS, SPICE MIXES AND DRINKS

Turmeric is a very versatile ingredient, not only for dusting on as a seasoning, but for creating basic sauces and ingredients to use throughout your cooking. In this chapter, discover tips for using turmeric in everyday cooking and learn how to make delicious oils, spice blends, sauces and more.

GARAM MASALA

1 tbsp sesame oil

1 clove

3 tsp coriander seeds

1 tsp dried red
pepper

1 tsp peppercorns

1 tsp fennel seeds

1 tsp ginger powder

3 tsp turmeric
powder

2 tsp coconut powder

1 tsp cinnamon
powder

Making your own signature spice mix can be both simple and rewarding. This blend was created by Kiran Vyas, an Ayurvedic chef who works at Tapovan in Paris. It can form the basis for a number of curries and soups, and can even be sprinkled on to salads.

Fry all the spices (leaving out the powders) in the sesame oil, stirring for five minutes until fragrant. Pour into a coffee grinder and add the spice powders. Grind. Seal the mix in a jar and store in a cool, dry place.

TURMERIC POWDERS

Turmeric gomasio

1 tbsp sesame seeds
1 tsp turmeric powder
1 tsp black pepper
Pinch of salt

Gomasio is an essential ingredient in any vegetarian kitchen, comprising toasted sesame seeds, salt – and a turmeric twist. Be as generous with the quantities as you wish – gomasio will keep for a couple of weeks. Sprinkle generously on vegetables or cereals for an instant dose of omega 3.

Dry fry the sesame seeds for a couple of minutes in a hot pan until they start to crackle. Pour out on to plate. Mix in the turmeric powder and pepper. Add a little salt. Store in an airtight jar.

Linseed and turmeric powder

2 tbsp flaxseeds
2 pinches sea salt
1 tsp turmeric powder
½ tsp black peppercorns

As with gomasio, this recipe is loaded with omega 3 fats, helping your stomach flora thrive. Make in small batches that won't oxidize.

Lightly heat the flaxseeds in a dry pan for two minutes. Add the salt. Once the aroma of the seeds has been released, pour mix into the coffee grinder. Add the turmeric powder and the peppercorns and grind. Store in an airtight jar.

TURMERIC OILS

Scented turmeric oil

**200ml/¾ cup olive
or sesame oil**

**1 tsp turmeric
powder**

**Black pepper
to grind**

Pour oil into a glass bottle. Sprinkle in turmeric
and pepper, stopper the bottle and shake well.
Sample the mixture and season to your taste
(being the stronger aroma, sesame oil tends
to drown out the more delicate turmeric).
Alternatively, dilute with extra oil. Use your oil
infusion to make hummus, chickpea salad or
roasted vegetables.

Turmeric dip

1 lemon

2 tbsp olive oil

2 tbsp rapeseed oil

2 tbsp soya milk

**1 tbsp soya sauce
or tamari**

**1 tsp turmeric
powder**

**Black pepper
to grind**

Rich in omegas 3 and 6, this zesty coloured dip
is perfect for guilt-free snacking. It's well worth
preparing a hearty batch, so that you have some in
reserve whenever you feel the desire to dip.

Juice the lemon and blend or mix everything
together well. Pour into a glass jar, screw the lid
down tightly and keep in the fridge.

MAYONNAISE

Sesame and turmeric mayonnaise

A delicious vegan-friendly alternative to mayonnaise, this sunny yellow condiment keeps for just as long as the real thing.

2 tbsp sesame paste (tahini)
1 pot soya or other yoghurt
1 tsp mustard
1 tsp turmeric
Black pepper to grind
Pinch of salt

Whisk the sesame paste with the yoghurt and the mustard. Season with turmeric and black pepper. Salt lightly.

Soya mayonnaise

With its lacto-fermented soya-cream base, this mayonnaise absorbs spicy heat and flavour remarkably well. Use it for sauces of every variety – even sweet ones. It is the perfect accompaniment to seaweed or vanilla.

1 tsp turmeric
Black pepper to grind
Pinch of salt
2 tbsp rapeseed oil
2 tbsp soya cream
1 tsp mustard

Mix the turmeric with a grind or two of pepper, a pinch of salt and the rapeseed oil. In a bowl, whisk the soya cream and mustard together. Then drizzle in the oil until you have a smooth sauce.

TURMERIC DRINKS

Comforting infusions

With its warm colour and peppery aroma, this drink is beautiful to look at – but perhaps serve in a glass mug to save your fine china from discolouration.

SERVES 1

250ml/1 cup water
½ tsp turmeric
Black pepper
  to grind
½ tsp ginger powder
1 tsp agave syrup

Dissolve the turmeric, pepper and ginger in the water, and bring the mixture to the boil. After five minutes, take off the heat, sieve and stir in the agave syrup.

Turmeric tonic

A chilled version of the above, this cooling turmeric tonic is the perfect drink for hot summer days. Sip throughout the day for instant refreshment.

SERVES 1

250ml/1 cup water
½ tsp turmeric
Black pepper
  to grind
½ tsp ginger powder
1 tsp agave syrup
1 or 2 tsp lemon
  juice

Dissolve turmeric, pepper and ginger in the water, and bring the mixture to the boil. After five minutes take the pan off the heat and strain. Sweeten with agave syrup and leave to cool. Finish with a squeeze of lemon juice.

Turmeric milk

This golden drink is delicately flavoured with warming spices and sweet honey – perfect for cosying up with on chilly winter nights.

Stir the turmeric and all the spices into the milk and bring to a boil. Reduce the heat and allow the mixture to simmer for five to ten minutes. Take off the heat and remove the cinnamon stick. Stir in a squeeze of honey to sweeten.

SERVES 1

250ml/1 cup of your milk of choice (almond, oat, soya, coconut or dairy)

½ tsp turmeric

1 cinnamon stick

½ tsp ginger powder

½ tsp ground black pepper

Honey or agave syrup to taste

Energizing elixir

This small shot packs a mighty citrus punch. Combining turmeric and ginger with a burst of vitamin C from the lemon, this elixir provides all you need to boost your immune system.

Wash the turmeric and ginger. Place both in a food processor along with a splash of coconut water. Blend until finely shredded. Strain the resulting pulp and mix the elixir with a squeeze of lemon juice. Add the black pepper. Serve in a small glass with a sprinkling of cayenne pepper.

SERVES 1

2.5cm/1-inch piece of fresh turmeric

2.5cm/1-inch piece of fresh ginger

2 tbsp of coconut water

1 lemon

Black pepper to grind

Cayenne pepper

SMOOTHIES

Kefir smoothie with red fruits

Kefir, labneh, lassi, buttermilk . . . these fermented milk drinks are part of a proud tradition that's too good to be confined to the history books. They aid digestion and are great for the health of your gut.

SERVES 1

4 small glasses of fermented milk
200g/1½ cups mixed red berries, fresh or frozen
4 tbsp agave syrup
1 tsp turmeric

Combine all ingredients in a blender. The turmeric gives fiery undertones to this healthy smoothie. Garnish with left-over berries and serve deliciously chilled.

Green smoothie

Green smoothies have become an emblem of clean, wholesome and healthy living – and deservedly so! They are a simple, delicious way to drink your five-a-day.

SERVES 1

2 peaches or mangoes
1 tsp turmeric
2 handfuls of young spinach or salad
1 banana

Begin by blending peaches (or mangoes) and turmeric together. Wash the spinach and add to the blender, little by little. Lastly, mix in the banana. Dilute to attain the consistency you like best. Drink immediately.

THREE

SALADS, SANDWICHES AND SOUPS

This chapter contains endless inspiration for turmeric-based starters, snacks and light meals. From quinoa-seaweed salad to cabbage soup, these dishes are deliciously simple and quick to prepare. Sprinkling turmeric into the mix adds a depth of flavour that will delight every diner at your table, providing an exotic new spin on each of these classic dishes.

FILLINGS AND SPREADS

SERVES 4

**2 tbsp flaxseeds
or powder**

1 tsp turmeric

**2 tbsp apple or other
fruit juice**

4 tbsp grated carrot

Salt to taste

**Black pepper
to grind**

Turmeric and flaxseed spread

Bored of sandwiches for lunch? Add spice to your slice with this quick and easy filling.

Grind flaxseeds to a fine powder using a coffee grinder or juicer (skip if using ready-ground seeds). Add the carrot, turmeric and season with salt and pepper to taste. Mix with your fruit juice of choice to create a dense, rich spread.

FOR ONE POT

5 grains cardamom

1 tsp black pepper

3 cloves

1 small onion

2 cloves garlic

**2 tsp freshly grated
turmeric**

**2 tsp freshly grated
ginger**

1 tsp cayenne powder

1 tsp salt

Olive oil

Turmeric paste with ginger

A traditional recipe with a modern twist, it's possible to create this paste using good-quality powders. But for the most vibrant result, you should shred fresh and succulent roots.

In a pestle and mortar, crush the cardamom, pepper and cloves (alternatively, use a pepper mill). Finely chop the onion. Crush or dice the garlic. Mix everything together in a small jar, adding enough olive oil to make a paste (you could use a small mixer too).

VEGETABLE CHIPS WITH TURMERIC

Whenever you're craving a snack, this recipe provides a satisfyingly swift solution – whatever vegetables you happen to have to hand.

Preheat oven to 200°C/400°F (Gas mark 6). Mix olive oil, turmeric and crushed garlic to make a marinade. Peel your vegetables and slice into 2cm/³/4-inch chips using a mandolin or grater. Brush chips with the marinade and place on a sheet of baking paper. Bake for about 15 minutes in the oven. Sprinkle chips with salt, pepper and turmeric powder. Serve warm or cold.

SERVES 4

2 tbsp olive oil
1 tsp turmeric
1 garlic clove
Vegetables: sweet potato, turnips, potato, beetroot, parsnip – take your pick

TURMERIC CRACKERS

Filled with an array of vitamins and minerals, these deliciously crunchy bites pack a powerful nutritional punch!

SERVES 4

50g/⅓ cup flaxseeds
50g/ ⅓ cup
** sunflower seeds**
200g/2 cups rye
** flour**
2 pinches sea salt
1 tsp turmeric
2 tsp honey
3 tbsp olive oil

Preheat oven to 150°C/300°F (Gas mark 2). Roughly grind most of the seeds in a mixer or coffee grinder. Leave a few seeds whole. In a bowl, mix the flour, salt, turmeric, grains and seeds. Make a well in the middle of the mixture, and pour in the honey and oil. Work this mix with your hands to make a ball. Its consistency should be slightly stickier than pastry for a tart, so add a little water or soya milk if needed. Roll out as thinly as possible on baking paper. Cut out the crackers into 3-by-5cm/1-by-2-inch rectangles. Lay them on lightly oiled baking paper. They need to be baked slowly and gently to attain the proper crispy crunch. Allow 30 minutes to ensure they're fully dehydrated.

TURMERIC AND SHIITAKE TOAST

SERVES 4

6 small dried shiitake mushrooms

2 tbsp olive oil

1 tsp turmeric

Black pepper to grind

1 shallot

Salt to taste

4 slices wholemeal bread

1 garlic clove

2 very ripe tomatoes

When you're too busy to shop, dehydrated shiitake mushrooms can be a life-saving cupboard staple. Simply soak them in warm water to release a world of rich earthy flavour and aroma.

Soak the shiitake mushrooms in warm water for 15 minutes. Once they're rehydrated, chop off the stalks, which are often quite chewy. Dice the mushrooms. Heat olive oil in a pan and season with the turmeric and a grind or two of pepper. Chop the shallot and add to the pan along with the mushrooms. Season with salt. Fry for 5 minutes, or until succulent.

Cover each slice of bread with fresh garlic and half a tomato. Toast under the grill. Top your toasts with the shiitake mix and serve immediately.

TURMERIC AND SHIITAKE CROQUE MONSIEUR

On days when you're feeling more indulgent, this flavoursome twist on 'turmeric and shiitake toast' is guaranteed to satisfy.

Prepare the shiitake mushrooms as for the toast to the left. Spread 4 slices of bread with tahini and the other 4 slices with miso paste. Spread four tahini slices with the shiitake mix and top each with a slice of miso bread to make sandwiches. Press tightly and brown lightly in a heated pan on both sides. Serve immediately, whilst your *croques* are still toasty.

SERVES 4

**6 small dried shiitake
mushrooms**
2 tbsp olive oil
1 tsp turmeric
**Black pepper
to grind**
1 shallot
**8 thin slices
wholemeal bread**
4 tsp tahini
4 tsp miso

TURMERIC QUINOA SALAD WITH NORI SEAWEED

SERVES 4

- 1 small glass quinoa
- 4 tbsp olive oil
- 1 tsp turmeric
- 1 lemon
- Black pepper to grind
- 125g/4 ounces smoked tofu
- 2 ripe tomatoes
- 1 avocado
- 1 lime
- 2 tsp nori

Pairing creamy avocado with nutty quinoa crunch, juicy citrus tang with crisp-and-cool nori flakes, this is a salad of delicious contradictions, all of them underpinned by the spicy warmth of turmeric.

Rinse the quinoa and place in a pan. Add twice as much water and cover with lid. Simmer for 20 minutes until all the water has been absorbed. Leave to stand.

Mix olive oil, turmeric, a squeeze of lemon juice and a few grinds of pepper to create your dressing.

Next prepare the salad. Roughly chop the smoked tofu and dice the tomatoes. Mix both with the quinoa. Stir in the dressing and leave to cool. Just before serving, peel and chop the avocado, and add to the mix with a squeeze of lime juice. Garnish with a generous sprinkling of nori.

PICKLED TURMERIC EGGS

MAKES 6 EGGS

6 hard-boiled eggs
300ml/1¼ cups
  cider vinegar
150ml/⅔ cup water
2 tbsp turmeric
  powder
2 tbsp sugar
1 tsp salt
½ onion
1 tbsp pepper

Requiring very little preparation, these pickled turmeric eggs are perfect for lunch on the go or as a swift starter. They keep for up to two weeks in the refrigerator and taste delicious.

Firstly, hard-boil your eggs. To do this, boil in pan for 8 minutes. Take off the heat, drain and leave to stand in cold water. Once they are cold enough to handle, peel off shells.

Meanwhile, add vinegar, water, turmeric, sugar and salt into a saucepan and simmer on a low heat. Stir in the sugar, letting it dissolve.

Dice the onion. Place onion, pepper and eggs in a glass jar. Next pour in the turmeric-vinegar mixture. Secure the lid, softly shake, and store in the fridge.

VEGETARIAN BOLOGNESE

For those looking to cut back on their meat consumption without compromising on flavour, this bolognese is the ideal solution.

Start by preparing your squash purée. Peel and chop the squash. Place pieces in a pan of water and bring to the boil. Simmer for about 20 minutes. Next, drain and mash with the back of a fork to attain a smooth purée-like texture.

Heat 2 tbsp olive oil in a wide pan. Skin and dice the garlic and add to the pan. Grind in the pepper and half of the turmeric. Dice the tomatoes and add to the pan. Leave everything to sweat on a low heat for 20 minutes. Take off the heat and mix in torn basil leaves.

Warm 2 tbsp olive oil in a separate pan. Chop the onion and add to pan along with the remaining turmeric and a few generous grinds of pepper. Add salt. Crush the tofu with the back of a fork; add the squash purée and tomato sauce and leave to reduce while you cook the spaghetti. When the pasta is almost cooked – to an *al dente* crunch – drain and mix with the sauce.

SERVES 4

500g/2 pounds squash
4 tbsp olive oil
1 clove garlic
Black pepper to grind
2 tsp turmeric
6 ripe tomatoes
Handful of fresh basil leaves
1 onion
125g/4 ounces tofu (smoked tofu works well)
300g/10½ ounces spaghetti
Salt to taste

GRATED TURNIP WITH PINK MASALA SALT

SERVES 4

FOR THE
MASALA SALT:

1 tsp turmeric

1 tsp caraway seeds

½ tsp nutmeg

Black pepper
to grind

2 tsp sea salt

1 tsp cardamom
powder

FOR THE SALAD:

250g/9 ounces
turnips (other
root vegetables
– squash, carrot,
beetroot, parsnip,
black radish,
celeriac – work
equally well)

2 shallots

1 apple

Juice of a lemon

Olive oil

Masala salt (see
above)

75g/½ cup sunflower
seeds

From fragrant florals – marigold, cornflower and lemon grass – to the complex smoky tones of cardamom, turmeric blends well with an incredible array of different spices. I adore experimenting with my own mixes – and pink masala salt is a favourite (see pages 20 to 23 for further inspiration).

FOR THE MASALA SALT:

Mix turmeric with caraway seeds, nutmeg, pepper, sea salt and cardamom, and save in a jar as your spice of choice.

FOR THE SALAD:

Peel the turnip and grate. Grate or finely chop the shallots. Grate the apple and mix all the grated ingredients together. Dress immediately with the lemon juice – to avoid discolouration – and then drizzle with olive oil. Season with the masala salt. Toast the sunflower seeds under the grill or in a pan, and sprinkle on at the end.

CABBAGE SOUP WITH MUSHROOM AND GINGER

SERVES 4

10 shiitake mushrooms
½ small cabbage
2 tbsp olive oil
1 tsp turmeric
Black pepper to grind
2L/8½ cups water
1 potato
5cm/2-inch piece root of ginger
1 tbsp miso

Shiitake, cabbage and ginger combine within this warming bowl of oriental goodness.

Soak the shiitakes in warm water to rehydrate. Slice the cabbage into thin strips. Warm the oil in a pan and season with turmeric and a grind or two of black pepper. Stir-fry the cabbage for a minute or two, and then add water. Dice the potatoes and add along with the shiitake mushrooms and the stock in which they've been soaking. Cover pan with lid and simmer for 40 to 45 minutes. Fifteen minutes before you take them off the heat, skin and mince the ginger. Add to the mix (if you don't like the idea of ginger shreds in your soup, you can add it to a tea strainer or a mesh bag and remove at the end). When the soup is ready, dissolve the miso in a few spoons of liquid. This will add a richly savoury flavour.

CARROT SOUP WITH FENNEL AND WALNUTS

The strong but complementary flavours here contrast with the sweetness of the carrots, which are high in potassium and vitamin C. The nuts can be varied according to the seasons, if you like. Fresh, wet walnuts are ideal but almonds also work well if you toast them first for a few minutes in a pan to release their natural oils.

Peel and dice the onion. Warm some oil in a pan and add the onion. Let it sweat quietly while you peel and roughly chop the carrots. Add them to the onions. Chop the fennel. Keep back a few fronds for the garnish and add the rest to the pan. Dice the potato, leaving the skin on. Mix everything together and add the turmeric. Bring a kettle of water to the boil and cover everything with 2 litres/8½ cups hot water. Leave to simmer for 30 minutes, then liquidise.

For the garnish, break up the walnuts, coriander and fennel with a few turns in a pestle and mortar to release the oils, then float them on top to serve.

SERVES 4

½ onion
Olive oil
3 medium sized carrots
¼ fennel
1 medium sized potato
1 tbsp turmeric
2L/8½ boiling water
Handful walnuts, shelled
Coriander, to garnish

CREAM OF SWEET POTATO SOUP

SERVES 4

500g/1 pound sweet potatoes
500ml/2 cups oat milk
1.5L/6⅓ cups water
2 tbsp oat flour
1 clove garlic
1 tbsp olive oil
1 tsp turmeric powder
Black pepper to grind

Every bit as versatile as wheat flour – but far less likely to aggravate sensitive stomachs – oat flour is a life-saving substitute for anyone trying to switch to gluten-free. Here it's used as a thickener, adding creamy texture to this comforting potato soup. And, unlike its wheaty counterpart, this light and lovely substitute is guaranteed not to weigh you down.

Preheat oven to 180°C/350°F (Gas mark 4). Peel the sweet potatoes and cut them into slices. Lay them in a tray and cover with oat milk and water. Bake in the oven for 30 minutes, or until the potatoes are soft.

Blend in a food processor. Pour the soup into a pan with the water and, over a gentle heat, stir in the oat flour. This will give your soup a deliciously thick and velvety texture. Leave to simmer for 5 to 10 minutes.

Meanwhile, in a bowl, combine crushed garlic clove with the olive oil and turmeric powder – beat well until properly mixed. Finish with a few good grinds of pepper. Drizzle this blend over your soup before serving.

FOUR

CAKES, PANCAKES AND CURRIES

While it is best known for its use in curries, turmeric is also an excellent addition to cake and pancake recipes. From carrot cake with turmeric to Brussels sprouts with lemon and spicy pancakes, the following recipes combine complex flavours with a healthy vegetarian twist.

CARROT CAKE WITH TURMERIC AND MISO SAUCE

SERVES 4

**FOR THE
CARROT CAKE:**

3 eggs
**200ml/¾ cup vegan
milk (rice, oats or
soya)**
**110g/1 cup chickpea
flakes or rolled
oats**
**750g/1½ pounds
carrots**
2 tbsp olive oil
2 tsp turmeric
Pinch of salt
**Black pepper
to grind**

**FOR THE MISO
SAUCE:**
**2 tbsp toasted
sesame oil**
2 tsp miso

Thanks to its light and airy chickpea base, this is a savoury cake for all seasons. Serve with a helping of pumpkin, leeks, stewed peppers – whatever is in season. Made with protein-rich eggs and pulses, this balanced meat-free meal is delicious eaten warm or cold.

FOR THE CARROT CAKE:

Preheat oven to 180°C/ 350°F (Gas mark 4). Start by mixing beaten eggs, milk and flour in a bowl. Let the mixture rest. Meanwhile, grate carrots. Heat oil in a frying pan and sprinkle in turmeric. Add carrot and pepper, and fry for a few minutes. Add salt. Mix in the batter and pour into a lightly oiled 23cm/9-inch loaf tin. Bake for 35 minutes. Allow to cool and serve in slices.

FOR THE MISO SAUCE:

Miso has a very strong savoury flavour which is only enhanced by the nutty tones of toasted sesame oil. Dissolve the miso with sesame oil, adding dashes of water until you attain the desired consistency. Then, it's good to serve. If you prefer something milder than miso, sesame mayonnaise may be more to your taste (see page 26).

LEMON-INFUSED BASMATI WITH CARROT CAVIAR

In this dish, the citrus zing of rice and the delicate aromas of vegan caviar combine in a single perfect pairing.

SERVES 4

FOR THE RICE:

200g/1 cup basmati rice

1 tbsp olive oil

1 tsp turmeric

1 tsp mustard seeds

Black pepper to grind

Juice of 1 lemon

FOR THE CARROT CAVIAR:

2cm/¾-inch piece root of ginger

3 carrots, grated (swap with celery, parsnip or pumpkin, depending on the season)

1 tsp turmeric

3 tbsp olive oil

Black pepper to grind

Salt to taste

2 tbsp yoghurt or kefir milk

1 tsp grain mustard

FOR THE RICE:

Rinse the rice and simmer in double the volume of water. When the rice has absorbed all of the liquid, cover and leave to stand for 20 minutes.

To make the lemon infusion, warm some oil in a pan. Sauté the turmeric, mustard seeds and pepper for a few minutes. Add the lemon juice and heat for a further few moments. Pour this mixture over the rice.

FOR THE CARROT CAVIAR:

Peel and grate the ginger and carrots. Gently heat the turmeric and oil in a frying pan. Season with pepper and salt. Add grated ginger, followed by the carrot a few minutes later. Leave mixture to sweat down gently for 15 minutes, then remove from heat. Whisk up the yoghurt or kefir milk, add mustard and blend with carrot-ginger mix to complete your caviar. Pour this mixture over the rice and serve immediately.

LENTIL GALETTE WITH TURMERIC AND FRESH HERBS

SERVES 6

110g/½ cup lentils (green or red)

1 tsp turmeric

1 tsp allspice (pepper, cloves, nutmeg, ginger or cinnamon)

Salt to season

200ml/¾ cup water

2 tbsp olive oil

2 tbsp herbs – mint and/or chives

1 clove garlic

2 tbsp goat's milk yoghurt

Loaded with protein, lentil pancakes provide a delicious base for any balanced vegetarian meal. With the use of a smaller pan, you can also fashion them into blinis, for truly tempting aperitifs.

Using a coffee grinder or a small blender, grind your lentils into a powder that is not too fine. Tip into a bowl and mix in spices and salt. To create your batter, add water and leave to soak for at least an hour. The consistency you need is slightly thicker than conventional pancake batter. You can adjust by adding more water. Oil a large pan and tip in the lentil mix to cover the whole base (you can always use leftover batter to make more pancakes). Fry for a few minutes, then flip it with a spatula and cook the underside. To prepare a sauce, mince up the herbs, dice garlic and mix into the yoghurt.

SPICY PANCAKES WITH LEMON BRUSSELS SPROUTS

Ideal for diners who remain sceptical of the Brussels sprout, this recipe centres around the classic combination of cabbage and ginger, spiked with vibrant citrus flavour. Cooking without water also makes all the difference!

SERVES 4

FOR THE PANCAKES:
1 egg
200ml/¾ cup rice or soya milk
150g/1¾ cups porridge oats
1 onion, diced
1 tbsp sesame seeds
1 tsp turmeric
1 tsp allspice
Black pepper to grind

FOR THE PANCAKES:

Beat the egg and milk together, and mix in all other ingredients. Leave to stand for 30 minutes – the longer you leave the batter to rest, the easier the pancakes will be to form. Drop spoonfuls of batter into a well-oiled pan. Gently fry the first side. Flip and cook the underside.

FOR BRUSSELS SPROUTS:

Preheat the oven to 180°C/350°F (Gas mark 4). Remove outer leaves from the Brussels sprouts if withered and cut a cross, about 1cm/3/4-inch deep, into the stem of each sprout to facilitate cooking. Prepare a sauce with minced ginger, olive oil, the juice of half the lemon, turmeric, and a few grinds of pepper. Season with salt and pour over the sprouts in an oven dish. Bake for 30 minutes. Squeeze the rest of the lemon juice over the Brussels sprouts and serve hot or warm, with the pancakes.

FOR BRUSSELS SPROUTS:
250g/9 ounces Brussels sprouts
5cm/2-inch piece root of ginger, minced
3 tbsp olive oil
1 lemon
1 tsp turmeric
Black pepper to grind

MUSTARD TOFU WITH SPICY PUMPKIN PUREE

SERVES 4

FOR THE PUREE:

1 medium pumpkin

1 tbsp almond powder

1 tsp cinnamon powder

1 tsp cumin powder

1 tsp turmeric

Black pepper to grind

Salt to taste

FOR THE TOFU:

250g/9-ounce block of tofu

4 tbsp mustard

2 tbsp soya sauce

1 tsp turmeric

Black pepper to grind

Yeast, to cover

2 tbsp vegetable oils

Like potato, tofu is a wonderfully low-maintenance ingredient and can be transformed into something truly delicious with just a little effort. Encased in a crispy coating of yeast, this recipe makes it positively irresistible.

FOR THE PUREE:

Deseed pumpkin and cut into pieces. Place the pieces in a steamer and cook over a gentle heat for 20 to 30 minutes.

Once the pumpkin is cooked, it is easier to remove the skin – peel it now. Mash the flesh with a fork or potato masher. Mix in all the spices and season with salt to taste.

FOR THE TOFU:

Divide block of tofu into two. To create a marinade, mix mustard, soya sauce and spices together. Baste the tofu on all sides. Smother tofu in a coating of yeast. Next, warm the oil in a pan and fry gently – paying close attention to keep the yeast from burning (it does so quickly).

CAULIFLOWER CURRY WITH PRUNES

SERVES 4

10 prunes

2 tbsp olive oil

1 tsp turmeric

Black pepper
   to grind

1 tsp allspice

1 pinch cayenne
   pepper

1 pinch cumin powder

2 small onions

1 tbsp mustard

1 small cauliflower

1 clove garlic

500ml/2 cups
   coconut milk

200ml/¾ cup water

250g/9 ounces
   smoked tofu

Bread or rice,
   to serve

Curry is turmeric's greatest gift to cuisine. The sweet-and-sour combination of coconut and prunes is also delicious.

Remove stones from the prunes. Warm some oil in a pan and add all the spices. Chop the onions and add them to the pan, along with the mustard. Break up the cauliflower into small florets. After a few minutes add them to the pan. Next, skin and crush the garlic. Add this to the pan too.

Pour on the coconut milk and the water. Dice the prunes and tofu, and add to the mix. Simmer gently for 30 to 40 minutes. Serve piping hot with a side of bread or rice.

FIVE

DESSERTS, SWEETS AND SORBETS

Turmeric works beautifully with a range of delicious puddings from tapioca with matcha tea and turmeric jelly to vegetarian sorbet. If you want to make some guilt-free treats then try out the bonbon recipes. The combination of sweetness and spice makes the following turmeric delights the perfect end to any meal.

TAPIOCA WITH MATCHA TEA AND TURMERIC JELLY

Matcha tea's vivid green powder is so fine it requires no preparation for cooking. Paired here with tapioca – poetically named 'Japanese pearls' in French – its colour contrasts beautifully with a sunny jelly topping.

FOR FOUR SMALL GLASS RAMEKINS:

35g/¼ cup tapioca

240ml/1 cup almond milk

100ml/⅓ cup water

1 tbsp matcha tea

2 tbsp agave syrup

FOR THE TURMERIC JELLY:

100ml/⅓ cup water

1g/1 tsp agar-agar

200ml/¾ cup lemon juice

1 tsp turmeric

2 tbsp agave syrup

FOR FOUR SMALL GLASS RAMEKINS:

Gently heat tapioca, almond milk and water together in a pan. Simmer for 15 minutes, stirring until tapioca beads become transparent. Take off the heat and stir in matcha and agave. Pour into shot glasses and leave to cool while you make the jelly.

FOR THE TURMERIC JELLY:

In a saucepan dissolve agar-agar in water. Bring to the boil and then simmer for no more than 30 seconds. Add lemon juice, turmeric and agave. Pour over the tapioca and leave in the fridge for at least an hour to set.

RED AND YELLOW MARBLE CAKE

SERVES 4

3 eggs
100g/½ cup cane
    sugar
1 tbsp soya yoghurt
3 tbsp olive oil
150g/1 cup rice flour
1 tsp bicarbonate
    of soda
1 tsp vanilla extract
1 tsp turmeric
8 drops of orange
    essence
1 small beetroot

A guaranteed showstopper, this marble cake owes its enchanting colour-scheme to beetroot and turmeric. Mix them together with gusto for maximum effect!

Preheat oven to 180°C/350°F (Gas mark 4).

In a bowl, pour the eggs, sugar, soya yoghurt and one tablespoon of olive oil. Whisk vigorously, folding in the flour and bicarbonate of soda as you do so.

Separate the mixture into two batches. Dilute the vanilla and turmeric with one tablespoon of olive oil. Add to one half of the cake mix.

To colour to the second batch, stir in a tablespoon of olive oil mixed with orange essence. Juice your beetroot and splash that into the mix. Line a 20cm/8-inch cake tin with baking paper and pour in the two batters irregularly to create the cake's gorgeous marble effect. Bake for 40 minutes.

TURMERIC RICE PUDDING WITH GINGER CHUTNEY

SERVES 6

1L/4¼ cups vanilla-flavoured rice milk (or coconut milk)

50g/3 tbsp crystallised ginger chutney

150g/¾ cup white rice (arborio or short-grain work well)

1 tsp turmeric

3 tbsp agave syrup

Pinch of cinnamon

Shreds of ginger add texture and vibrant bursts of flavour to this entirely vegan rice pudding. Refrigerated in yoghurt pots, it has a long shelf-life . . . so that you can enjoy exotic breakfasts and desserts days after you prepare them.

Hold back a good glass of the rice milk. Cut the ginger into small pieces. Wash the rice.

Combine ginger and rice with what remains of the rice milk. Simmer on a low heat for 35 to 45 minutes. Take off the heat and add the final glass of rice milk. Mix together and cover. Blend the turmeric with the agave and use to sweeten the rice mix. Add a pinch of cinnamon if required.

VEGETARIAN SORBETS

Silken tofu – a softer, milder variety than used elsewhere in this book – provides welcome relief from dairy products and lends this sorbet its deliciously creamy quality. Though both recipes require an ice-cream maker, the results are more than worth the investment!

BOTH SERVE 6

2 lemons
400g/14 ounces silken tofu
1 tsp turmeric
100ml/⅓ cup agave syrup

3 or 4 vanilla pods
100ml/⅓ cup water
375g/1⅔ cups goat's milk yoghurt
100ml/⅓ cup agave syrup
1 tsp turmeric

Agave, lemon and turmeric

Finely grate lemons to obtain the zest. Drain the silken tofu and whisk vigorously with the turmeric, agave syrup, lemon zest and the juice of both lemons. You can do this by hand or using a blender. Once you've obtained a smooth, silky mixture, put into an ice-cream maker for 30 minutes. Enjoy immediately or store in the freezer for another occasion.

Vanilla sorbet with turmeric

Split and scrape out your vanilla pods. Put the seeds and pods in water and bring to the boil. Take off the heat and leave to cool, allowing the flavour to infuse. Pass the water through a strainer, discarding the vanilla, and then mix in other ingredients . Run through ice-cream maker for 30 minutes.

BONBONS – SWEETS THAT DO YOU GOOD

My usual base for these bonbons is fine flaxseed powder fresh from the coffee grinder, but flax meal or powdered flax provide equally delicious – and healthy – results.

ALL SERVE 4

4 tbsp flaxseeds

2 tsp turmeric

Black pepper
    to grind

3 tbsp agave syrup

4 tbsp coconut flakes

4 tbsp flaxseeds

2 tsp turmeric

Black pepper
    to grind

3 tbsp agave syrup

2 tbsp crushed
    almonds

4 tbsp flaxseeds

2 tsp turmeric

Black pepper
    to grind

3 tbsp agave syrup

1 drop bergamot
    essential oil

Coconut bonbons

Grind the flaxseeds in a coffee grinder to a fine powder. Stir everything but the coconut flakes together and knead into small balls. Roll in coconut flakes to coat and keep in the fridge.

Almond bonbons

Grind your flaxseeds to a fine flour. Mix everything except the crushed almonds and roll into small round balls. Dust with crushed almonds and keep chilled.

Bergamot bonbons

Grind the flaxseeds to a fine flour. Mix with other ingredients and roll into small balls. Keep in the fridge.